East Point, Nahant

Through Time

GERALD W. BUTLER
CAPTAIN, MASSACHUSETTS STATE GUARD

Former Curator of Fort Warren and Fort Independence
Boston Harbor and Fort Rodman in
New Bedford, Massachusetts

America
Through Time®
ADDING COLOR TO AMERICAN HISTORY

To my daughters, Heather, Tara and Alanna, shown above at Lackland Air Force Base in Texas, February 1999, my son, Michael, my parents, Mr. and Mrs. Gerald F. Butler of Nahant, Massachusetts, my uncles and grandfathers who served in the Spanish American War, trenches of France in World War I and the Army Air Corps and Armored Forces during World War II and Korea. Tara served in the U. S. A. F. during Operation Iraqi Freedom and Operation Enduring Freedom

It is a thing of no great difficulty to raise objections against another man's oration - nay, it is an easy matter; but to produce a better in its place is a work extremely troublesome.

Plutarch c. AD 46 - 120

America Through Time is an imprint of Fonthill Media LLC
www.through-time.com
office@through-time.com

Published by Arcadia Publishing by arrangement with Fonthill Media LLC
For all general information, please contact Arcadia Publishing:
Telephone: 843-853-2070
Fax: 843-853-0044
E-mail: sales@arcadiapublishing.com
For customer service and orders:
Toll-Free 1-888-313-2665

www.arcadiapublishing.com

First published 2019

ISBN 978-1-63500-095-5

Typeset in Mrs Eaves XL Serif Narrow
Printed and bound in England

Contents

INTRODUCTION

Nahant is located on the northern flank of Boston, Massachusetts, having the distinction of being the smallest community in the Commonwealth. The two-by-four-mile peninsula juts into Boston Harbor, and at the easternmost tip lies East Point. This rugged land mass is one of the most beautiful scenic areas in New England because of its spectacular jagged cliffs and sweeping ocean views. Additionally, the exposed cliffs at East Point offer geologists a plethora of wonders and its deep water is a boon to marine scientists.

During the Spring of 1005, Nahant was said to have been the resting place of Thorvold, the Norseman, following a shoreline exploration and fierce battle with Native Indians. Another area in Nahant, known as Bayley's Hill, may also lay claim to this fact, in addition to areas in Hampton, New Hampshire and Norway. In the early 1600s, Nahant's thick forests were toppled and used for building homes and structures in nearby Lynn. The deforestation then allowed abundant pasture areas for farmers, resulting in East Point becoming recognized as "Ram Pasture."

The remainder of the 1600s were spent in court contesting ownership of the lands. As it was part of Lynn, the area was hotly contested and eventually lotted in 1706. East Point then became divided and passed from common land to individual landowners. Toward the late 1700s, entrepreneurs began to view the value of the exquisite views that East Point offered. A small hotel was established, later being replaced by a massive, more commodious structure, known as the "Great Hotel," built between 1823 through 1825. East Point then became an extremely popular fresh air and healthy resort for the socialites of Boston. After a successful thirty-year period, the hotel faltered, and mysteriously burned in 1859. Shortly afterward, new investors purchased the land, constructing elegant mansions, or "cottages" as they were known by the owners. The entrance to East Point is defined below.

In 1898, East Point was utilized by the Massachusetts Volunteer Militia as a signalling and subaqueous mining station for defense of Lynn harbor and the southern limit of Boston Bay. It is at this period that the military history of East Point commences.

1

Earliest Times

East Point Primaeval: Originally the land mass now recognized as East Point was designated "Ram Pasture," following the deforestation of the peninsula. Because of the richness of the soil, the land was extensively used by farmers from nearby Lynn to allow their cattle and stock to feed. The solitary issue presented to the farmers was the hours of feeding were limited to the nature of the tides. A narrow sandbar separated Nahant to the mainland and at high tides and storms, it often became an island. Another concerning factor to farmers were the wild, carnivorous animals that roamed the peninsula. Farmers carried weapons in the event wolves began to encircle flocks, and at one point, professional militia men were assigned to the task. When most of the trees were felled by woodsman's axe, the problem of wolves diminished. In 1631, the tip of East Point became recognized as "Ram's Pasture" as it was an ideal location for cattle and sheep to peacefully graze and be protected.

THE FIRST HOTEL IN NAHANT: The Nahant Hotel was established at East Point, shown above. Thomas Perkins and William Paine, both of Boston, purchased East Point in 1821, to build a luxurious hotel that opened in June 1823. The hotel proved popular amongst socialites of Boston as it boasted all the newest amenities to make a visitor comfortable. Below: center left defines where the hotel stood.

HOTEL ALTERATION: In 1852, Paran Stevens acquired the hotel and added massive extended wooden wings, giving the entire structure a length of 400 feet, capacity of 300 rooms and dining for 600. The hotel was immensely popular with Bostonians, dignitaries and visitors from abroad. The new hotel, shown above with a color variant below, became recognized as the "Great Hotel." On September 12, 1861, the hotel mysteriously caught fire and within two hours it was completely destroyed.

2

THE ESTATES

EAST POINT: The first "cottage" constructed at East Point was the residence of Senator Henry Cabot Lodge, shown at left while relaxing at Nahant. Upon completion, it was named *East Point* and it was an extraordinary structure, shown below. The present-day location of the structure is forward of the 16-inch gun emplacement, *Battery John B. Murphy*, and to the front of "Lodge Beach."

LOWLANDS: Following the demise of the Nahant Hotel, John Ellerton Lodge purchased East Point, dividing the land between his son, Henry Cabot Lodge, and his daughter, Elizabeth, who married George Abbot James. Construction commenced in 1868, using the finest granite, stone and exotic woods. The "cottage" was occupied in 1871. Above, the cottage, *circa* 1965, and below, an interior view.

LOOKING TOWARD EAST POINT: Forty Steps Beach as it appeared in 1900. Left, the billiard house of hotel remains, later converted to Senator Lodge's library. Adjacent is Senator Lodge's cottage East Point, and to the right are ancillary buildings. To the far right is the James cottage, Lowlands. The James estate, purchased by Harmon Elliott in 1928, remained in place through the outset of World War II.

An Artist's Interpretation: The Cliff Walk gained great popularity, especially on a lovely sun-drenched Sunday afternoon. Above is The Cliffs at Nahant, North Shore, Massachusetts, the first of two beautifully rendered illustrations by William Thomas Smedley (1858-1920). Boston, with its faint plumes of smoke, may be observed in the far distance, while below is a postcard of the favored site.

A MOST POIGNANT ILLUSTRATION: On the Coast of Nahant, the second of two Cliff Walk illustrations was completed in 1897 by the popular artist and painter, William Thomas Smedley. The eloquence and simplicity of the cliff walk at East Point remains remarkable. The walk circumnavigated the entirety of the cliff area at East Point, passing on the periphery of the large, elaborate estates on the point.

ANOTHER PORTRAIT OF THE CLIFF WALK: Some sections of the original Cliff Walk remain in *situ* at varying locations throughout East Point. Unfortunately, much was destroyed due to weather and construction. Paths and stairs were carefully placed as not to interfere with the majestic beauty of the area. Left is a preserved staircase while below is a stormy sea seen from the walk.

3

SPANISH AMERICAN WAR

SPANISH ARMADA TO INVADE: Raiders were a threat to the eastern seaboard in 1898 while in Boston, militia units were called into federal service. The first unit to serve at East Point was the New England Guards, later replaced by elements of the First Regiment Massachusetts Heavy Artillery. Senator Lodge provided areas for military apparatus while General Paine allowed the encampment on his property. Above, the New England Guard band pose while the former camp area is below.

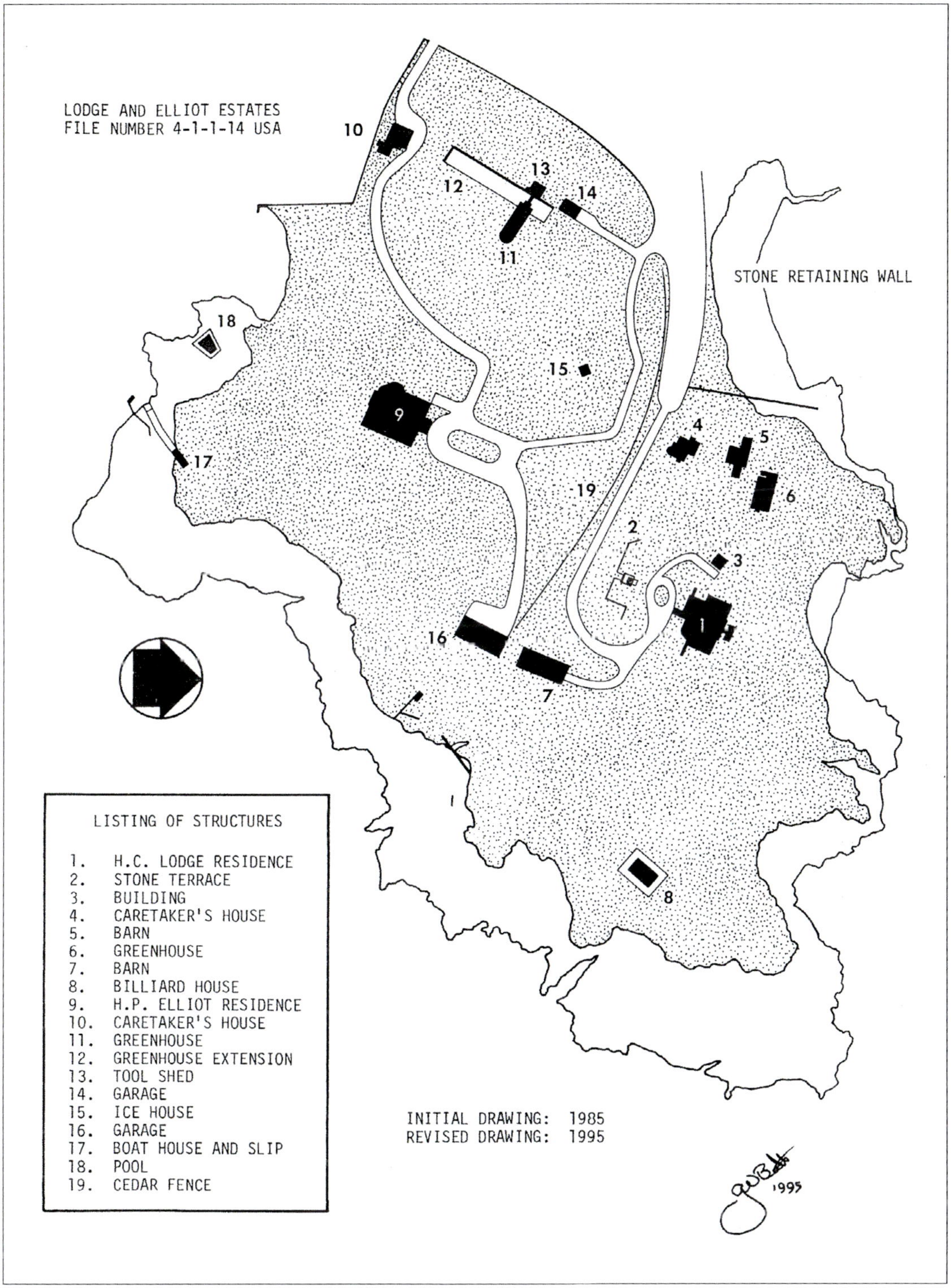

PLAN OF THE ESTATES: Above is shown the entirety of East Point showing all residences, sheds, pools, houses, buildings and greenhouse. The division between Senator Lodge's estate and Harmon P. Elliot's estate is indicated by the cedar fence, designated by number 19. U.S. Army map 4-1--1-14.

MANNING THE STATIONS: The most important factor when detachments arrived at East Point, Nahant, was to establish guard posts and signalling systems. The signal stations relayed communication between Gloucester and Boston. The line illustration below is an Infantry sentinel while at the bottom two relaxed officers posed with nearby signal flags.

ENDLESS TRAINING: Although the personnel manning the defenses in Nahant were mostly technical, they also had to be fit to completely fulfill the role of infantrymen. This included manning small caliber weaponry, Gatling guns, and to be able to defend against Spanish raiding parties. Above, the troops are drilling on a soft-sand beach while below is Long Beach in Nahant at the present day.

CAMP LIFE: Above: an officer and two soldiers preparing for formal guard duty, attired in field or fatigue dress, and full march order. When the New England Guards were stationed at the East Point area, the encampment was designated *Camp Lodgebank*, and later, *Station East Point*. Below is the former-encampment site on General Paine's property.

LEAVE ONLY FOOTPRINTS: United States Army and Naval victories were cause for celebration as the War of 1898, or the Spanish American War, drew to a close. The citizens of Boston, both north and south shores, and the townspeople of Nahant, were jubilant. On July 25, 1898, the military personnel departed, leaving no indication of trenches or a camp site and marched to Fort Pickering in Salem.

4

WORLD WAR I

A STRATEGIC LOCATION: East Point was recognized as a superior observation and signalling station for the Coast Defenses of Boston. A wooden "watching station" was created at the tip and a powerful searchlight was mounted nearby to illuminate the harbor. Below, a guard mount at the entrance to East Point with Castle Rock in the distance. The site appears identical at present.

A POWERFUL SEARCHLIGHT: With permission from Senator Lodge, the searchlight shown to the left was installed at East Point at the outbreak of World War I. Its primary function was to illuminate unidentified or enemy naval vessels attempting to enter the Port of Boston during the hours of darkness.

Below: The 60-inch searchlight, with a range of twenty-five miles, was concealed in a shed during daylight hours, and was mounted on a rail system that manually rolled up an incline to the middle of East Point to its position. The operating position is shown below.

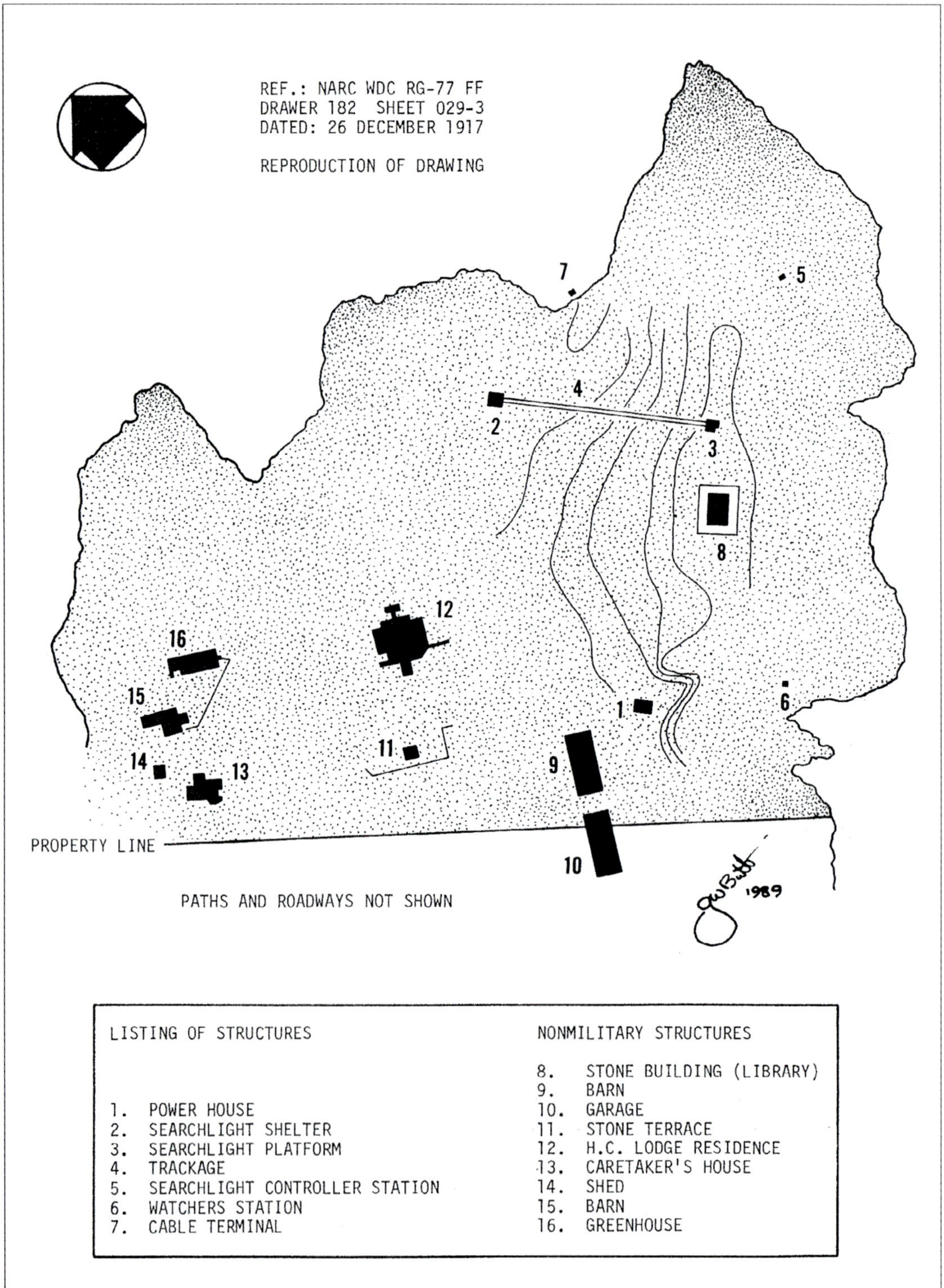

AN ORTHOGRAPHIC PLAN: Showing the area utilized on the Senator Lodge estate during World War I for a temporary 60-inch surveillance searchlight, power plant, rail system and watcher's stations.

5

Nahant Anti-Submarine Laboratory

A Means to End the War: During World War I, the most important development from Nahant brought new and efficient means for anti-submarine detection. In February 1917, the U.S. Navy created a committee to devise a way to detect submarines by subaqueous sound waves. Due to East Point's deep water, the laboratory, recognized as the Nahant Anti-Submarine Laboratory, was situated upon the estates of General Charles J. Paine and Mrs. Knyvet W. Sears. Above is the site test stable and individual laboratories, while below is a recent image of the area.

UNRELENTING RESEARCH: Initial construction of the facility was completed in April 1917, five days after the United States declared war on Germany. Under direct control of the U. S. Navy, the Submarine Signal Company, Western Electric Company and the General Electric Company Plant at Lynn all contributed to the system. Above: an aerial, and below, a ground capture of the NASL.

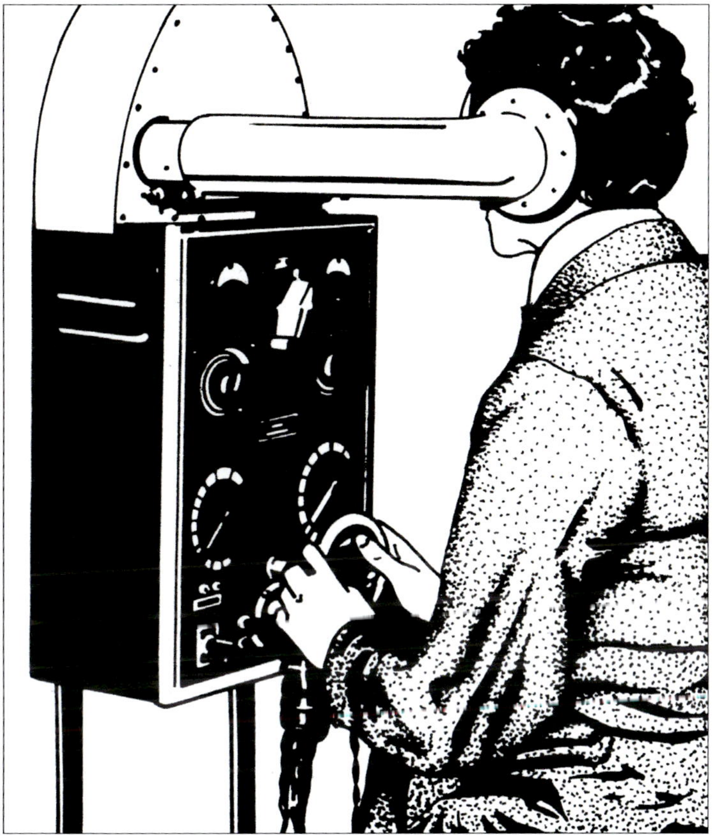

Unrelenting Testing: Hours of tests resulted in a device that could be lowered into the water and "listen" for underwater sounds such as submarine propellers. The device was accepted and mass produced for the United States and Allied navies. Above: A compensator device. Below: A typical United States Navy Submarine Chaser equipped with a Nahant anti-submarine detector.

6

SECRET EXPERIMENTS

REVOLUTIONARY LIGHTS: Following World War I, new experiments were carried out at East Point with permission of the landowners. The first series of tests involved mobile searchlights. The mobile light shown below, *G.E. Lynn Design Type Number 4-A*, was made by the General Electric Company in Lynn and extensively tested. Bottom: the general area where mobile searchlights were tested.

A unique searchlight, used for artillery and coastal artillery illumination, the Strauss mobile-tower searchlight, is shown at left. The searchlight was considered the first self-propelled 36-inch searchlight designed and utilized for the United States Army. Below is the area at East Point that the mobile-tower searchlight was tested. Gun 2 of Battery Murphy and Lodge Beach are visible.

ANOTHER EXPERIMENT: Another searchlight experiment conducted at East Point consisted of a small mobile searchlight. The 36-inch field-type searchlight was an extremely powerful unit, mounted on a static carriage-mount and considered the first lightweight mobile searchlight. Above is the searchlight and below are the three points at East Point where testing was conducted.

AN "AERIAL BOMB": East Point was also involved in a secret remote-control aircraft, manufactured by the Curtiss Aeroplane Company. Tests involved an advanced-design remote controlled aircraft, known as an "aerial torpedo," or "flying bomb." Originating from a flying field in Gloucester, the unmanned aircraft flew to Nahant, circling Broad Sound, and returned to Gloucester. A group of scientists at the tip of East Point evaluated the test and were in communication with Gloucester in the event their assist was required. Above is the Curtiss "aerial torpedo," and below, the tip of East Point from where the experiments were observed.

HAMMOND'S DIRIGIBLE TORPEDO: Shown above is the remote-control "Dirigible Torpedo," equipped with an array of antennas that responded to shore signals directing it to a specific target. Development began in 1911 at Gloucester, with selected operational sites throughout Boston Harbor, including East Point. Packed with high explosives, it was guided to an enemy warship at night when their searchlights were activated, and during daylight the Dirigible Torpedo was guided to an enemy warcraft by protected and camouflaged shore stations. Below is one of the selected and protected anchorages for the Hammond craft.

HAMMOND'S SECRET TORPEDO SYSTEM: The last experiment concerning remote control at East Point was the "Hammond Torpedo Control System for Coast Defense." A series of torpedo batteries, or "nests," were proposed for East Point, consisting of multiple reinforced concrete tubes, similar to that of submarines. The airtight chambers pointed seawards, with provision to be reloaded via an underground tunnel. A protected underground transmitting and surface viewing stations were positioned to control the torpedoes after launch. Additionally, disappearing antennae was used for torpedo control, while protected underground facilities were to be created for storage, workshops and testing. Above is a shipboard system and below is a proposed site for the Hammond system.

7

World War II

Most Secret Proposal: East Point was selected prior to World War II as a strategic site for the newest and most powerful coastal defense weaponry extant. Upon Declaration of War, members of Battery "G," 9th Coast Artillery Regiment (HD), manned and guarded the East Point station with patrols, and machine gun nests, shown below. Bottom: the area today.

THE FIRST REQUIREMENT: Although East Point was selected for new systems, it was defenseless in December 1941. Shown in upper image, 155 mm guns firing at Fort Dawes in Winthrop which were later towed to East Point and emplaced at the tip of East Point, adjacent to the Billiard Hall. Below: A 1952 Town of Nahant aerial view of the gun site. Gun 1 is in the circle at upper right, center.

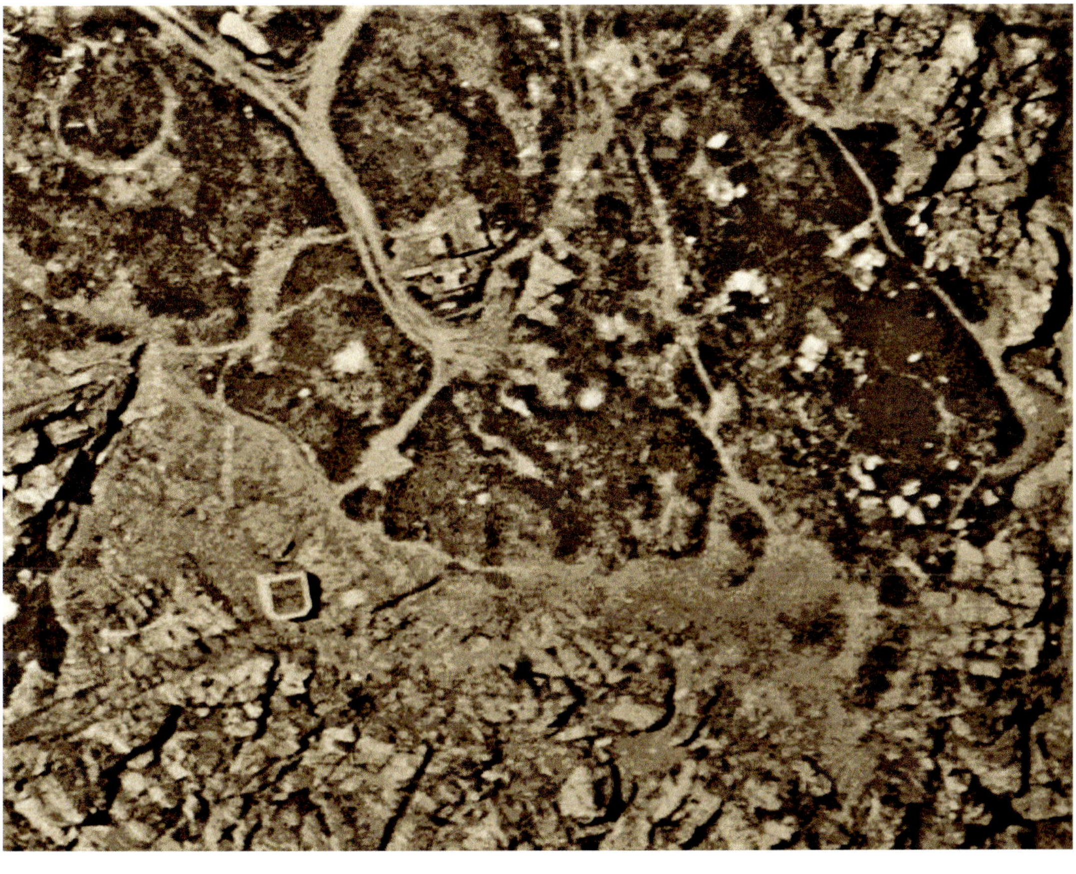

PANAMA MOUNT, GUN 1: By spring 1942, two concrete Panama Mount gun mounts were established at East Point. The design would enable the weapon to fire at any given target within a 360-degree radius, not limiting it to a specific field of fire. The upper capture depicts the gun ready for action while the lower image illustrates the gun and emplacement with camouflage in place.

AMMUNITION MAGAZINES: The upper photograph was taken during winter 1942 at East Point. In the distance may be viewed the observation station at the Mifflin estate and Spouting Horn, both under construction. The magazines, and limbers for the 155 mm guns are located near the tip of East Point, indicated by shortened trees. Below are off-duty gunners.

PANAMA MOUNT, GUN 2: Looking under the camouflage netting at the gun mount. The 155 mm gun is resting upon the circular raised segment of the Panama Mount with trails on the 360-degree steel traverse rails. The wooden wedge platform was placed to assure gunners smooth transition of ammunition whilst loading. Below, the gun platform partially covered by winter growth.

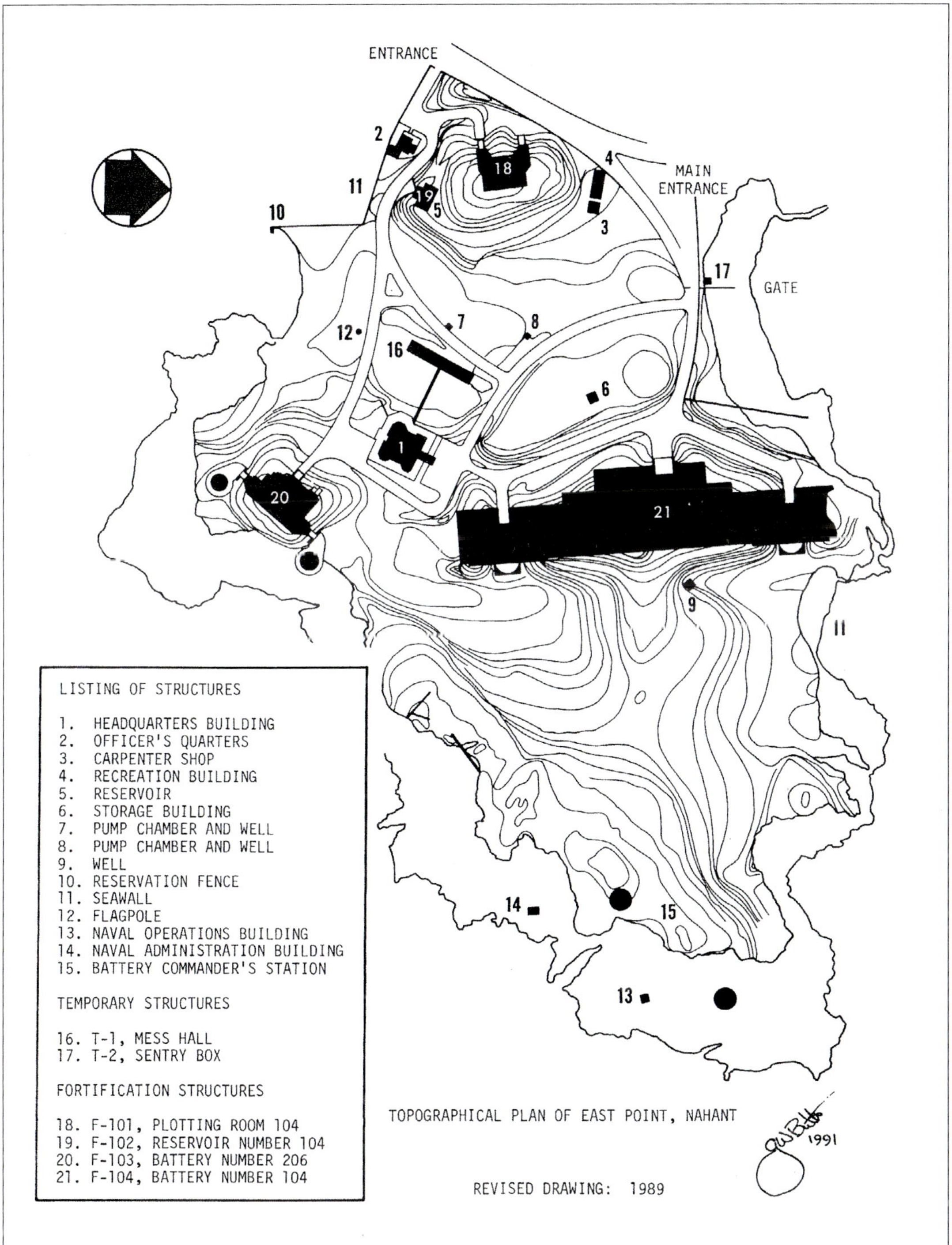

REVOLUTIONARY GUN BATTERIES: The new layout for East Point consisted of an extraordinary 16-inch casemated gun emplacement, a smaller 6-inch shielded rapid-fire gun emplacement and protected supportive facilities including a plotting and switchboard room, and a revolutionary protected water reservoir and fire-fighting system. Above, a layout of the systems proposed and as built.

8

Battery 104 John B. Murphy

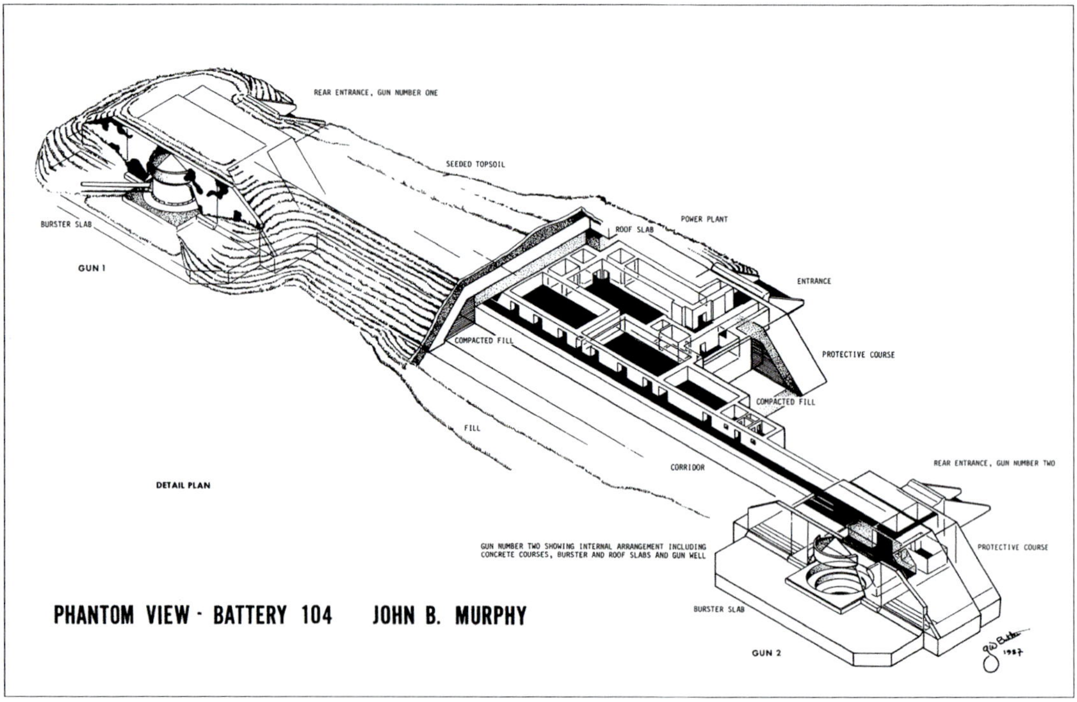

CONSTRUCTION IN FORCE: Construction of all new systems at East Point was constant, regardless of weather. Following clearing and rock removal, the huge foundation for the 16-inch gun emplacement was laid out. Steel supports were forced into bedrock, forms were created and concrete, type "C" was poured. The completed gun emplacement measured 625 feet long and 160 feet wide.

THE ULTIMATE GUN EMPLACEMENT: The 16-inch gun emplacement was an advanced gun battery, and consisted of two massive, long-range 16-inch guns mounted on modernized carriages along with supportive systems and a power-plant, all within a hardened reinforced concrete casemate. Construction began during winter 1942. Sadly, the first landmark demolished was Senator Lodge's residence.

EMPLACEMENT CONSTRUCTION: Construction commenced on January 23, 1942, with a scheduled completion date of January 23, 1943. The gun rooms were begun first. The gun rooms each measured 52 feet long, 31.5 feet wide and 15 feet high. Top: Gun Room Number 1 under construction, and beneath, the burster slab in place prior to earth cover placement.

THE COMPLETED EMPLACEMENT: One of the largest systems installed within the gun battery was the power plant. Known as Power Plant M1, the system used three large diesel-electric generators rated at 375KVA with triplicates of supports systems and an overhead rail crane, mounted on concrete supports. Top: power plant as designed and below, the power plant today, transformed into a classroom.

INSTALLING THE GUN TUBE: The final unit to be installed was the gun tube. The upper capture depicts a typical 16-inch gun tube in the gun room hall with a relieved and resting rigging and hauling crew. A series of rollers and winches were used to manually bring the tube into the emplacement. The lower image is the present rear entrance to gun 1 of *Battery John B. Murphy.*

AMMUNITION SERVICE SYSTEM: Each 16-inch shell weighed 2,240 pounds. A unique delivery system was developed to bring the heavy projectiles from the Shell Room to the gun proper which consisted of overhead rails and switch units. The top image represents the arrangement in the gun room, while the bottom photograph shows the system prior to salvage.

COMPLETION: Designated *Battery Number 104* when completed, the gun battery was named in honor of John B. Murphy, a former United States Army Coast Artilleryman. The projectile was capable of a 25.6-mile range and with a booster charge, the range was extended to 29 miles. Later, Gun Number 1 was fitted with special 4-inch thick shields. Top: Gun Number 1 in 1944 while below at present.

CAMOUFLAGE MEASURES: *Battery John B. Murphy* was extensively camouflaged by means of disruptive paint and large net systems that covered both gun and gun room. When the camouflage nets were extended, the entire face of the gun room appeared to become a hill. The upper image illustrates the netting in place. In the lower right, personnel are barely visible. The lower image captures the gun room as it appears presently.

PROOF-FIRING: Upon *Battery John B. Murphy's* completion and acceptance to the Coast Artillery, the 16-inch guns were proof-fired and calibrated as required. The former Lodge estate was located between the gun rooms. All of the trees were cut to allow the guns a visual and clear firing zone. The lower frame vividly captures the moment that a 16-inch gun fires.

TERMINATION: *Battery John B. Murphy* was last fired on Friday, June 13, 1947, and declared surplus in May 1948 due to advances in aircraft and missiles. Major items to include engines and generators were removed and stored at Boston Army Base, while the 16-inch gun tubes and carriages were salvaged on site as shown at a similar system in California, while the lower photograph indicates the empty gun pit and recoil well.

PLOTTING ROOM 104

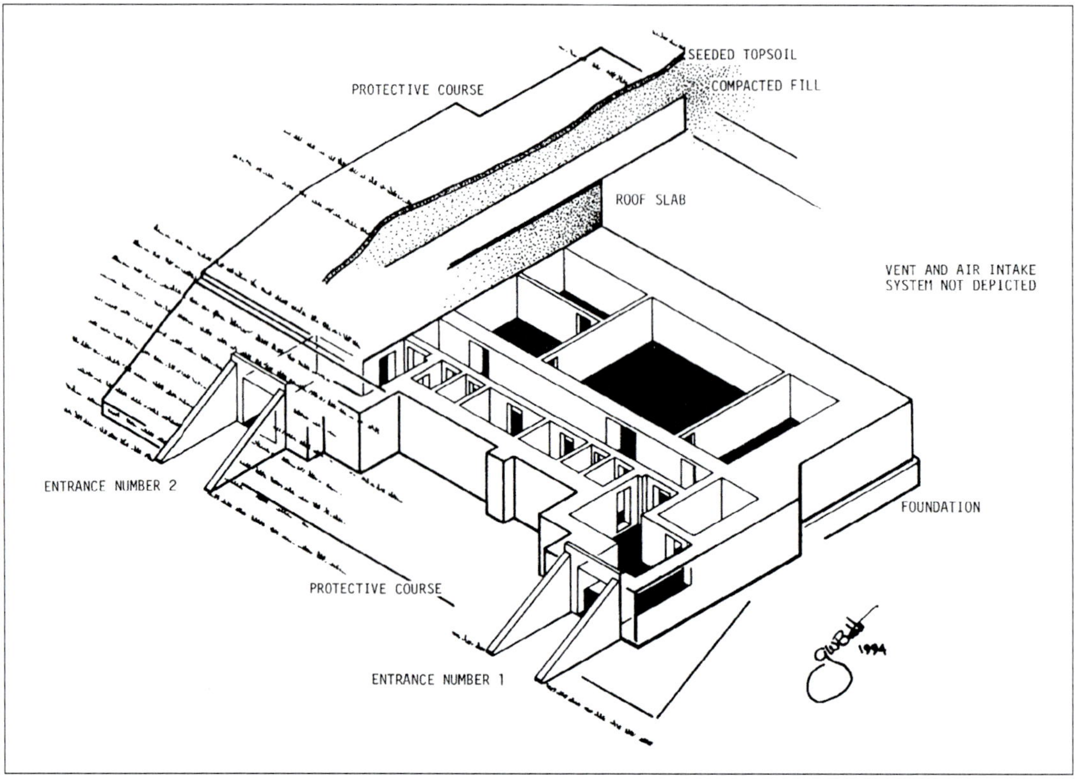

NERVE CENTER OF THE GUN BATTERY: Plotting Room 104 was established a distance from the gun battery proper due to vibration and noise levels when the 16-inch gun battery fired. Construction began in 1942, coinciding with construction of *Battery Murphy* and was completed during the summer 1943. A phantom view of Plotting Room 104 is shown below. The completed casemate was 118 feet long, 93 feet wide and 27 feet high.

ENTRANCE TO THE CENTER:

Plotting Room 104 was situated within feet from Swallow Cave Road and to the rear of *Battery John B. Murphy*. The underground unit was accessed by two gated doors with Air Locks at each entry point, both of which led directly into the hall that contained a plotting room and a telephone-switchboard room. Below is Entrance Number 1 while the bottom image is the hall, with Plotting Room to right.

Plotting Room Importance: Plotting Room 104 was established to track enemy warcraft attempting to penetrate the Port of Boston. Data from the observation towers along the north and south shores of Boston would be transmitted to the plotting room then compiled with other factors to accurately track a target. Data was displayed on a large semi-circular plotting board as shown below, and the chamber today.

GUN DATA COMPUTER: The most important device in Plotting Room 104 was the Gun Data Computer M-1, shown below. This large, mechanical computer measured 7 feet long, 3 feet wide, and 4 feet, 6 inches high. Data transmitted from observation stations were automatically fed into the computer resulting in the correct azimuth and elevation to point the guns. The lower image portrays the colorful chamber at present.

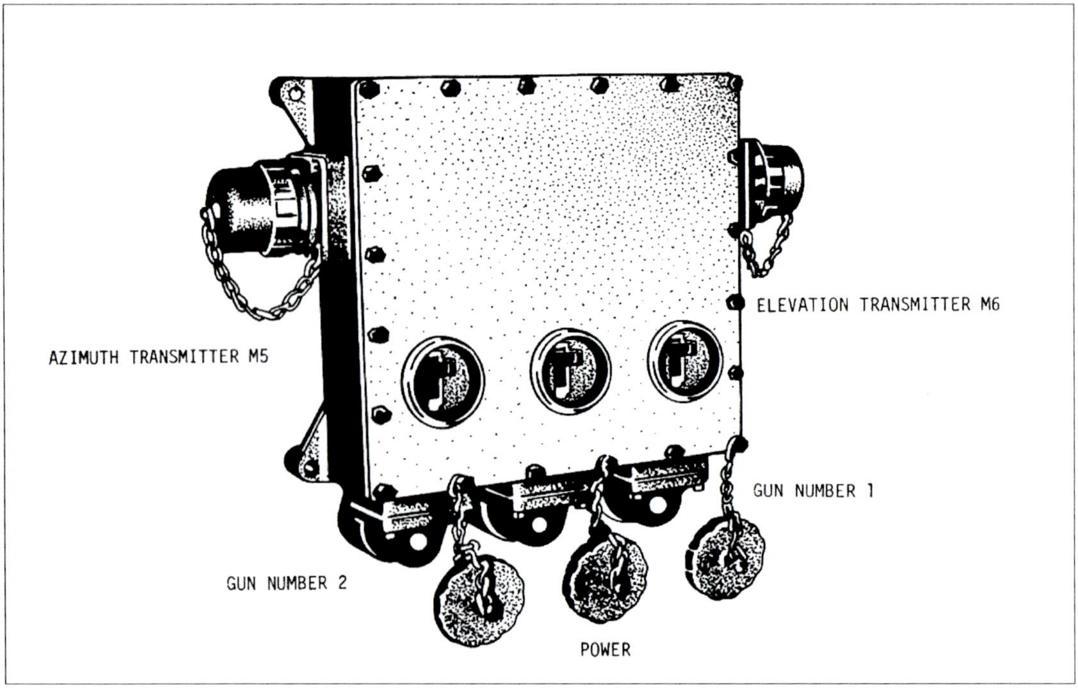

GUN DATA COMPUTER SYSTEMS: The Gun Data Computer M-1 digested the incoming data which became mechanically computed and then fed this data to the azimuth and elevation transmitters. This data was transmitted to the guns by underground cabling to aim the 16-inch guns and fire. Mounted on the wall of the plotting room, the transmitters are shown above while the lower capture shows the wall where the units were mounted.

RESERVOIR NUMBER 104

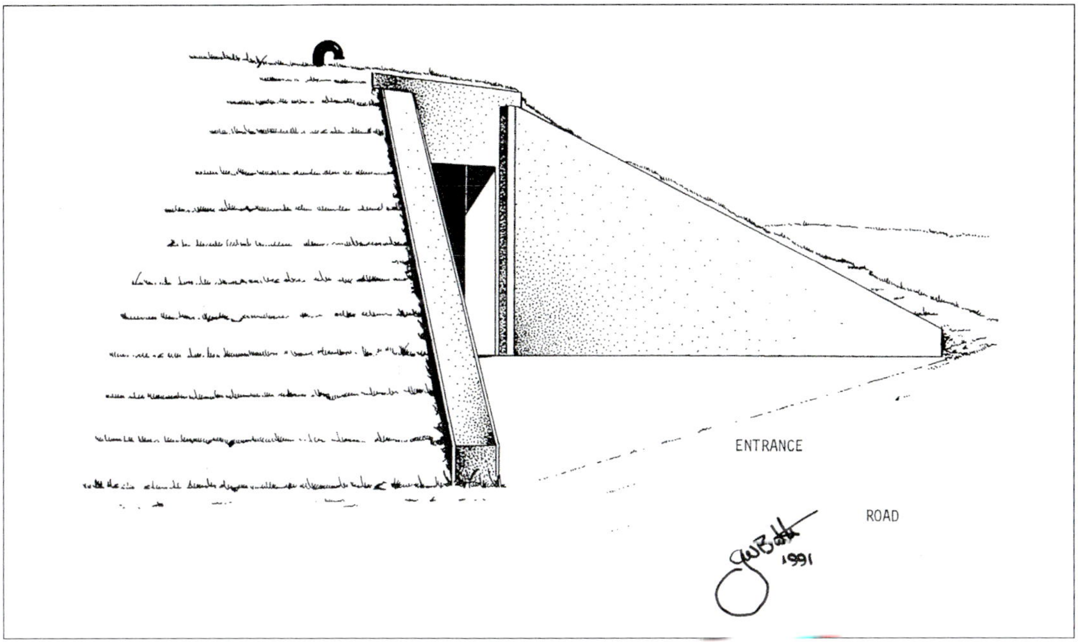

WATER SUPPLY: Officially designated Reservoir Water Supply System for Battery 104, it was situated a short distance from Entrance Number 1 of Plotting Room 104. It consisted of a pump house, shown above, and two 25,000-gallon concrete reservoirs. Each reservoir measured 20 feet squared with a 9-foot depth. Additionally, the Pump House contained a domestic water supply reservoir. Bottom: The Pump House at present.

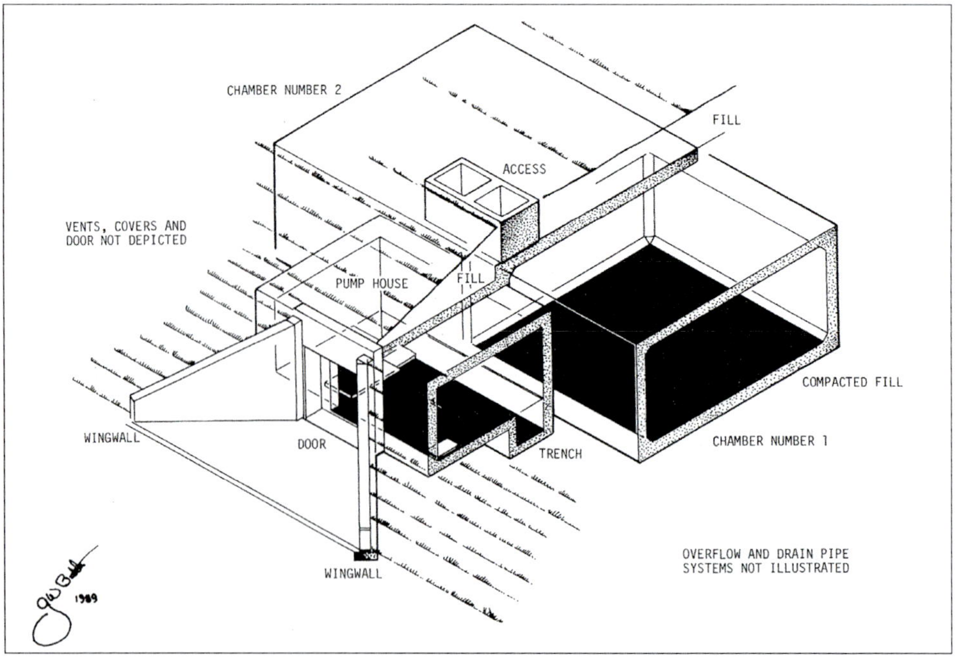

PUMP HOUSE: The Pump House was equipped to supply water from a commercial supply or to function in isolation. The primary purpose was to supply fresh water to the gun battery engine cooling systems, while a domestic interior tank supplied chlorinated water for the garrison. In addition, two on-site wells were used. It was also equipped with a powerful Dayton-Dowd Company high-pressure pump for firefighting.

9

BATTERY NUMBER 206

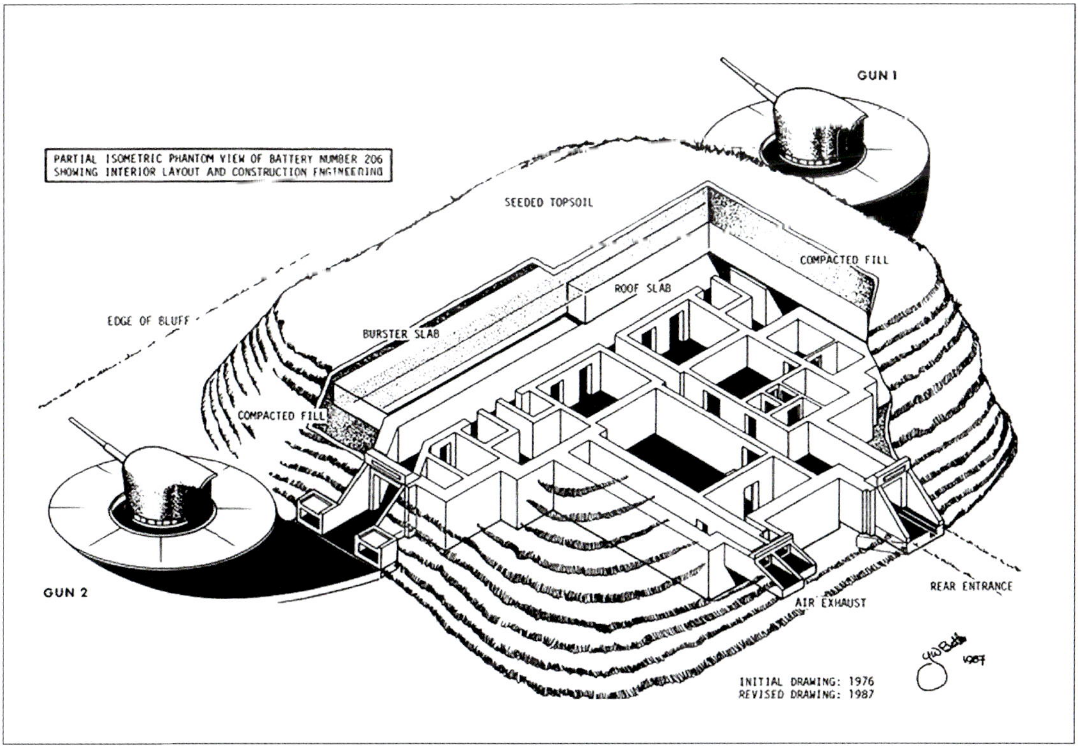

RAPID-FIRE DEFENSE: Battery Number 206 consisted of two six-inch guns mounted within two shielded turrets. Between the exterior guns, a protected casemate of reinforced concrete was established containing a power plant, plotting room, communications and ammunition service. A phantom view of Battery Number 206 is shown below. The completed casemate was 255 feet long and 122 feet wide.

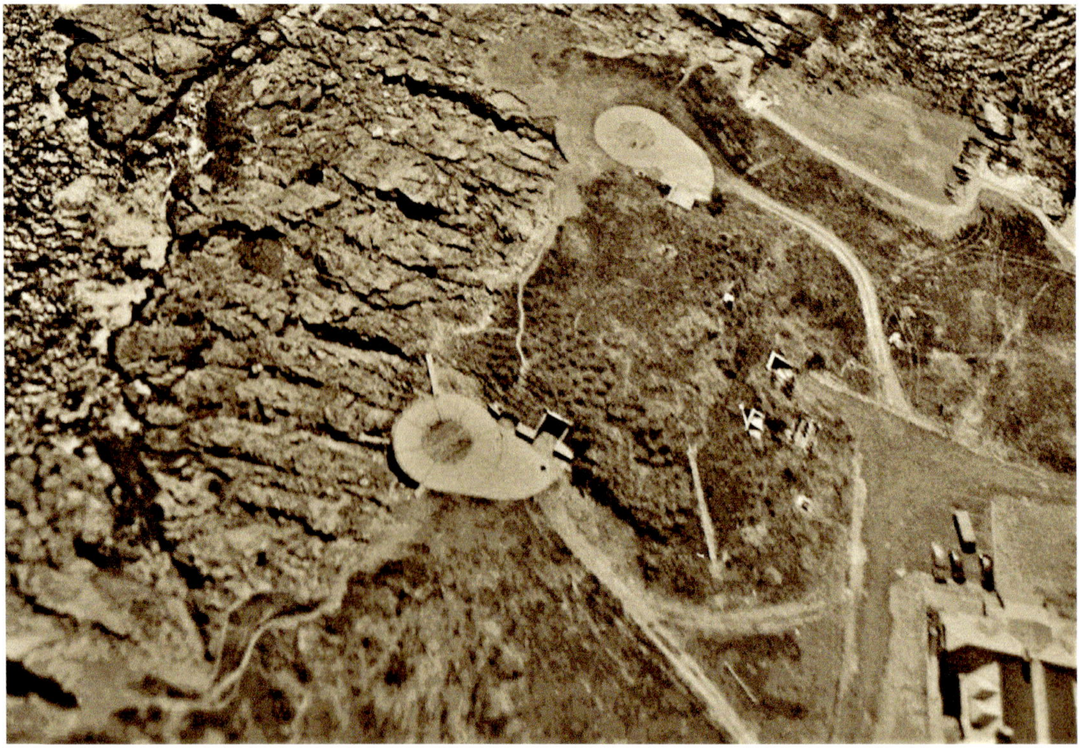

AERIAL VIEW: The aerial image illustrates the outlay of the 6-inch gun emplacement. Taken in April 1952, activity in the casemate indicates storage of 90-mm projectiles and .50 caliber ammunition for the antiaircraft gun battery at the site. Below is a later aerial capture taken from seawards of the emplacement showing erosion and landfill over Gun Number 2 as required for the Nike Ajax fire control system.

GUNS AND SHIELDS: A 1944 photograph of Battery Number 206 highlighting Gun Number 2. At the time of this image, erosion was controlled by military personnel on a frequent basis. After a hurricane in 1944, the Number 2 gun necessitated repairs to its gun block. The upper image shows Gun Number 2 in 1944, while the lower image represents the gun block showing its colorful present-day appearance.

PLOTTING ROOM: Within the emplacement was the important Plotting Room. A series of devices, including a plotting board apparatus for determining range and other devices to direct gunfire, were installed. The chamber was gas-proof, allowing personnel to function during a gas attack. Below is the plotting board in a similar 6-inch gun battery, Battery Number 210, while the bottom image shows the chamber at present.

POWER PLANT: A representation of Power Plant M4 in Battery Number 206 consisted of three 125KVA diesel-electric generator sets with all supportive equipment including air start, reservoirs, fuel supply and three evaporative condensers. Exterior diesel tanks provided fuel when needed. The upper image illuminates the three generating units while below is a typical distribution panel of a "200-series" power plant.

GUN ACCESS: Access to the magazines of both Gun Number 1 and 2 were through the main corridor of the emplacement of which the powder and projectiles were stored. In addition, the main corridor had storage rooms and air compressor rooms that were used to eject gas and powder remnants from the gun tube when fired. Below, Gun Number 1 entrance under construction, and bottom, as it appears at the present date.

THE 6 INCH GUN: The 6-inch gun was a rapid-fire gun by a well-drilled crew. The gun and shields were mounted on a 360-degree platform which enabled the gun crew to strike at land targets. The shield was 6.5 inches thick, while the gun had a range of 14.8 miles. On September 14, 1944, a severe hurricane struck the Boston area, damaging Gun Number 1, upper image, while, below, Gun Number 2 suffered damage to the gun apron.

THE "EXAMINATION BATTERY": Battery 206 was the examination battery for Boston Harbor. The guns were manned continuously and tasked to fire within thirty seconds of alert. The carriage was of special design, allowing it manually to track a target moving at 30 mph at a distance 1.7 miles. Battery 206 was to be named in honor of Major M. S. Holbrook, but this was not enacted due to secrecy. The upper photograph shows the author with an identical gun while the lower view shows the gun block as it is today.

10

Naval Operations

THE FINAL SECRET: Nahant utilized another secret system to detect submarines from a shore station. Two reinforced structures were built by Richard White & Sons Company for the Navy to detect enemy submarines attempting to penetrate the Port of Boston. Completed in mid-May, 1942, the Operations Building was transferred June 22, when it began operating. Above: The station in 1942 and, below, as it is today.

German Submarine U-87: A fascinating story concerns the German submarine *U-87* and its crew during June 1942. Under command of Kapitänleutnant Joachim Berger, *U-87* patrolled the eastern seaboard. Before laying six TMB mines off Boston Harbor, the undersea craft rested on the seabed off East Point, Nahant from 8 p.m. June 11 through 8 a.m. on June 12. The Captain noted in his War Diary, "The city of Boston is hardly darkened. The beacons burn as in peacetime." Additionally, "I intend to lay 4 mines off the north part of the northeast entrance, 2 mines off the east part." The mines remained in place until after the war when U. S. Naval Intelligence reviewed war logs and messages. *U-87* had been resting either on top or quite near the magnetic loop array from Nahant, but remained undetected as the loops were not activated at that time. *U-87* sank five vessels, including the S.S. *Port Nicholson,* a cargo ship carrying 71 tons of platinum ingots, gold, and industrial grade diamonds for payment of lend-lease aircraft and other war material. The *U-87* also took part in five war patrols, but was sunk on March 4, 1943, west of Leixoes.

The upper two images depict Kapitänleutnant Joachim Berger and the emblem of *U-87*, while the lower indicates a Type VIIB submarine.

ADMINISTRATION BUILDING: The second structure constructed was the Administration and Power Building. This low structure was divided into an administration section and a power generating station. Both units began operation on July 17, 1942, while the entire system at Nahant was designated *Naval Unit 1-D*. Above, the station in 1942 showing ingenious camouflage measures to blend into surrounding rock formations and as it is at present.

HIGHLY SECRET SYSTEMS: The Operations Building contained a magnetic loop detector apparatus that, via two subaqueous cables, Loop C and D, had a loop of 4.5 miles long and projected far out into Massachusetts Bay. Placed on the seabed, no vessel could attempt to sneak into Boston Harbor undetected. Below is a station with three fluxmeters in place, while below is a recent view of the Nahant station showing the fluxmeter base.

RADIO-SONO-BUOY: Following modifications to the Operations Building, a new design of submarine detection means was installed. Designated the Radio-Sono-Buoy, the first unit was installed and operational on July 3, 1942. Radio-Sono-Buoys were placed inboard of the magnetic loops and would indicate speed and type of vessel that crossed over the loop cables. The receiver was mounted in the building while seven buoys were eventually operated from the Nahant station. Two naval watchstanders, one shown below, were on duty in the Operations Building at all times.

ALERT!: Between July 1942 through May 1945, there were four alerts called by the Harbor Defenses of Boston, but only one alert called by the Nahant unit. During a frigid winter evening in 1943, the Radio-Sono-Buoys began silencing, one at a time. A battle alert was called and the entire harbor now was active with gun batteries manned while radar and searchlights swept the areas. At first light, a patrol boat discovered the reason—the antennas of the buoys became heavy with ice and turned upside down, negating transmissions.

CLOSURE: At 8:00 a.m., May 29, 1945, U.S. *Navy Unit 1-D* at East Point ceased operation and was phased out. Below: a rare photo of the manning crew at the Administration and Power Building. Bottom: a recent capture of the interior. When Navy equipment was being salvaged, a large Navy crane was brought to the site. Upon departure, it "accidentally" severed the main power line into the Army installation as a parting gesture.

11

DURATION

GUN BATTERIES OPERATIONAL: By early 1944, all of East Point's gun batteries and systems had been officially transferred to the Coast Artillery and proof-fired. New buildings were erected, including a mess hall and a small guard house. Although the threat of Axis capital warships ended, the reality of submarines, torpedo boat and rocket attacks remained. Upper image: mess hall, 1952 and below, the Elliott estate, 1945.

WORRISOME, INDEED: Toward the end of World War II, German scientists developed a series of "wonder weapons" to use against Allied forces. One of the most troubling was the midget submarine. Operated by one man, the midget submarine was ferried across the Atlantic atop a regular *U-Boat* and released offshore with intent to penetrate a harbor and sink ships. One such instance occurred in Portsmouth, New Hampshire, but the operator asphyxiated, and the miniature submarine eventually sank at the harbor entrance. The German Air Force developed a long-range bomber, iconically termed the *Amerika Bomber,* capable of reaching New York and returning to its base. Simultaneously, the German Navy developed a towed platform to launch V2 missiles against major Atlantic cities including Boston and New York. Fortunately, all threats were countered. Above: The *Amerika Bomber* and below, the miniature *Molch*-class submarine.

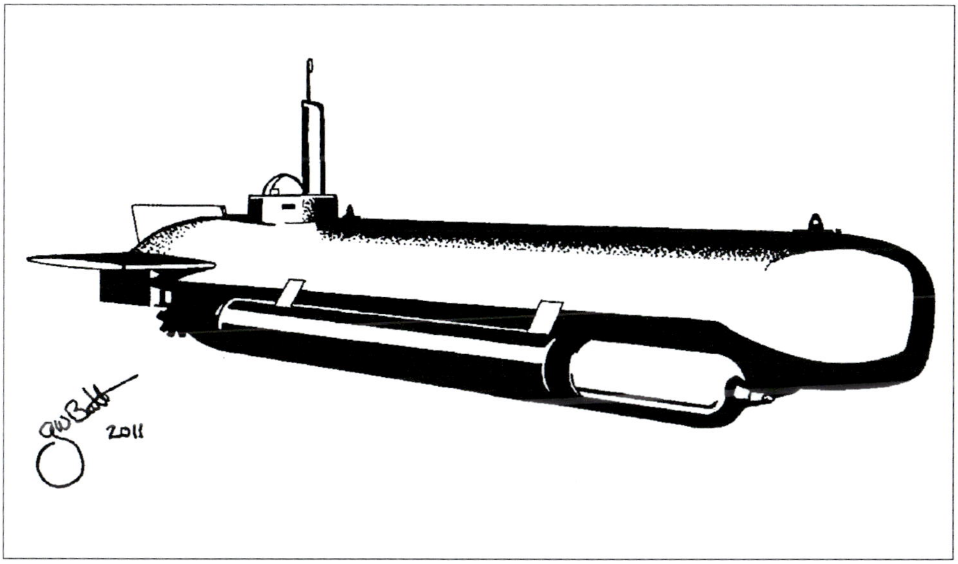

Frankie Fontaine

An Outstanding Comedian: During the war, an enlisted man named Frank Fontaine, at right, was assigned to the East Point Military Reservation. His duty normally consisted of being an observer in the two observation towers shown below. During an alert, PFC Fontaine would mimic noises of radios, birds and other characters. Upon the occasion of proof-firing the massive 16-inch gun battery, a group of high-ranking officers and dignitaries were in the upper observing level of his tower. PFC Fontaine began his mimics and imitations. The General was concerned that there was a commercial radio on and immediately sent his aide to investigate. The aide found no radio and returned to inform the General. Later the sounds of cats fighting, cartoon sounds of birds twittering and barking dogs commenced. Before firing the big guns, the noises quickly abated. Frankie Fontaine later became a regular comedy act on television's *Jackie Gleason Show*.

Termination

Maintenance Status: The war had ended, and East Point was placed on maintenance status. Furthermore, all of Nahant's weaponry were obsolete and were to be salvaged. It then became known that East Point was to be named either *Fort Lodge*, in honor of Senator Henry Cabot Lodge, or *Fort Holmes*, in honor of Oliver Wendell Holmes. In 1943, *Fort Holmes* was chosen, but due to wartime secrecy, never applied or named. Below, left: Senator Henry Cabot Lodge and right: Oliver Wendell Holmes.

12

THE KOREAN WAR

ACTIVATED ONCE AGAIN: At 8:15 a.m. on January 30, 1952, the telephone rang at the Nahant Police Station. The call was to inform them an Army convoy was headed to East Point with purpose of activation and reoccupation. Shortly thereafter, the site received four 90-mm antiaircraft guns with ammunition and supportive radars. Above: Land clearing forward of the 16-inch gun battery. Below: Four 90-mm guns in place.

MAIN ENTRANCE: The entrance to the Nahant Gun Site is identical to the estates of the 1800s, as shown above. The Army retained the full-grown trees with the only alteration being that the lower four feet of each tree was painted white as a warning to drivers. Beach stones were gathered along the road and in true military fashion, painted white. The lower image indicates changes to the entrance, the stone pillar remains.

SEARCHING THE SKIES: Battery "A," 704th Antiaircraft Gun Battalion (90-mm), took station at East Point during Spring 1952. The battery consisted of four officers and 125 enlisted men and four M1A1 90mm guns, an SCR-584 Radar, an acquisition radar, and two "quad 50" antiaircraft machine guns mounts in turrets. The upper view depicts the 90-mm M1A1 antiaircraft gun, while below are three happy gunners ready for pass.

REDESIGNATION: In June 1953, when the 704th AAA Battalion was deactivated at nearby Fort Dawes in Winthrop, the unit became redesignated Battery "A," 605th AAA Battalion (Static-90 mm). The unit was equipped with the new 90-mm M2 antiaircraft gun, and the new T-33 acquisition and fire control system. Above, the acquisition radar, called "bathtub radar" by the battery, while below is the tracking radar.

"The Life of Riley": The garrison at East Point enjoyed the location, atmosphere and beauty of East Point. All personnel were quartered in the former Elliot estate, while the Mess Hall had been brought up to Army requirements. Above: The "cottage," as used during the Korean War era, indicating the driveway used by the military. Bottom: the driveway and road at present.

MESS CALL!: The "TO" (Theater of Operations or temporary building) Mess Hall was constructed during World War II, but used again during the reoccupation during the Korean War and longer. When a new, modern Mess Hall was constructed at Fort Ruckman, or Bayley's Hill, for the Nike-Ajax system, the contents of the older mess hall were salvaged and stored at Fort Banks in Winthrop. The image to the left shows troops of the garrison lined up at the front door waiting for the noon meal. Below: Interior of a typical Army Mess Hall. Bottom: Front door of the East Point Mess Hall prior to demolition.

ONLY IN SPIRIT: On November 4, 1953, members of "A" Battery, 605th AAA Bn., posed for a group portrait at the side of the former Elliott cottage. This group remained on site manning the 90-mm antiaircraft guns until the Nike-Ajax guided missiles were operational. A number of Non-Commissioned Officers and enlisted men transferred to the new Nike system. Below: Members of Battery "A" prepare for an evening pass.

13

THE COLD WAR

REDESIGNATED: In July 1954, East Point became designated *Site B-17, Special AAA, Boston Defense Sector.* Site B-17-C was the control site at Bayley's Hill while the launcher site, B-17-L, was at East Point. The Wexler Construction Company was chosen as the contractor. Although two locations were proposed, the tip of East Point was chosen, resulting in a tremendous amount of fill required, as noted in the two images below.

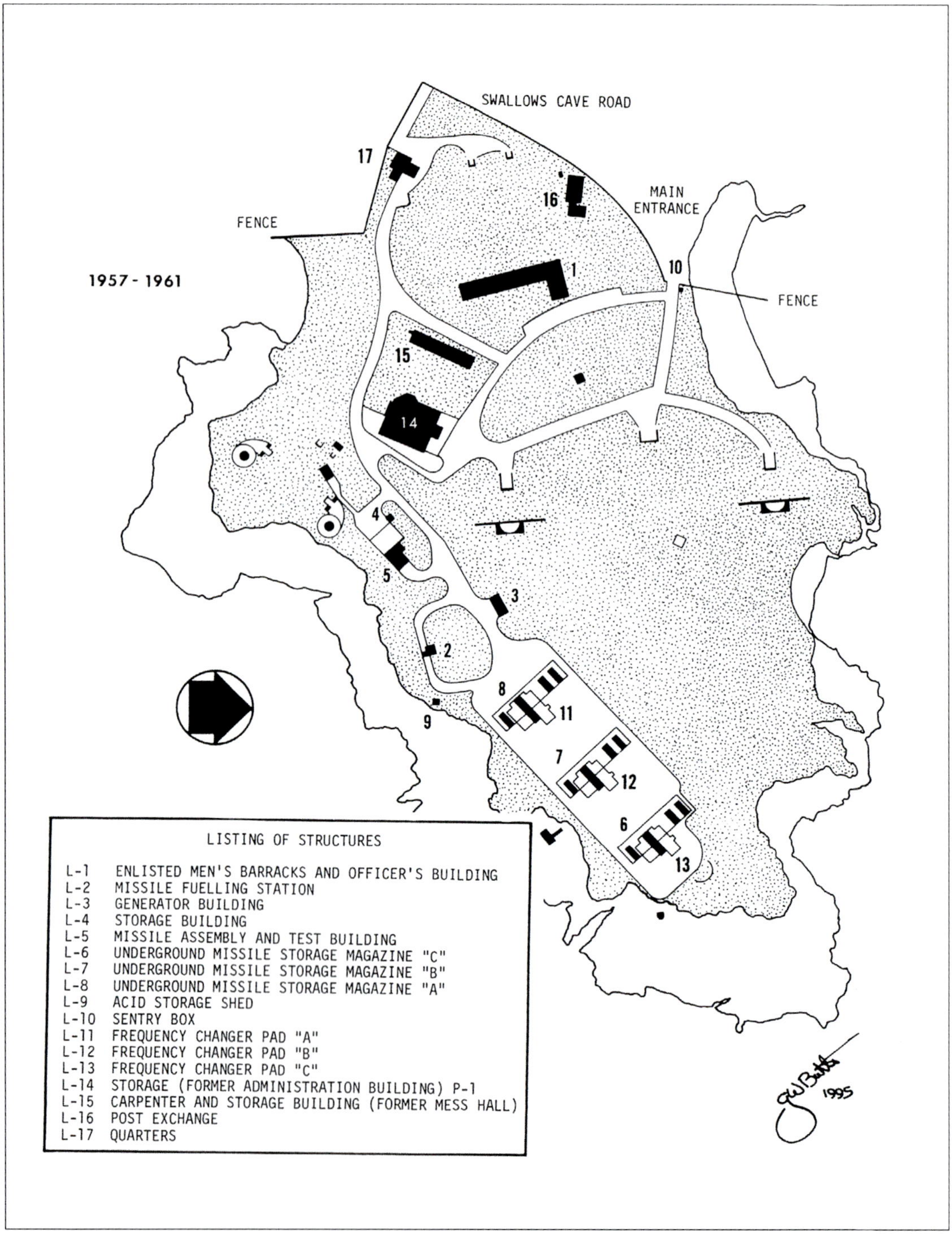

New Systems: The Nike-Ajax missile system modified the East Point landscape in many ways. The entire tip now contained three Underground Storage Missile Magazines, while half of Battery 206 was now under earth cover and fill. Additional buildings were erected for power, testing, arming and fueling the missiles. The map below indicates all systems, buildings and structures associated with the missile systems.

MISSILES ON THE SURFACE:
To the left are Nike-Ajax missiles being inspected and maintained at East Point launcher site. Maintenance was performed on site every day in all weather. When an alert was called, all missiles had to be ready for firing. Below are Nike-Ajax missiles on their surface launchers during a drill, ready to be fired.

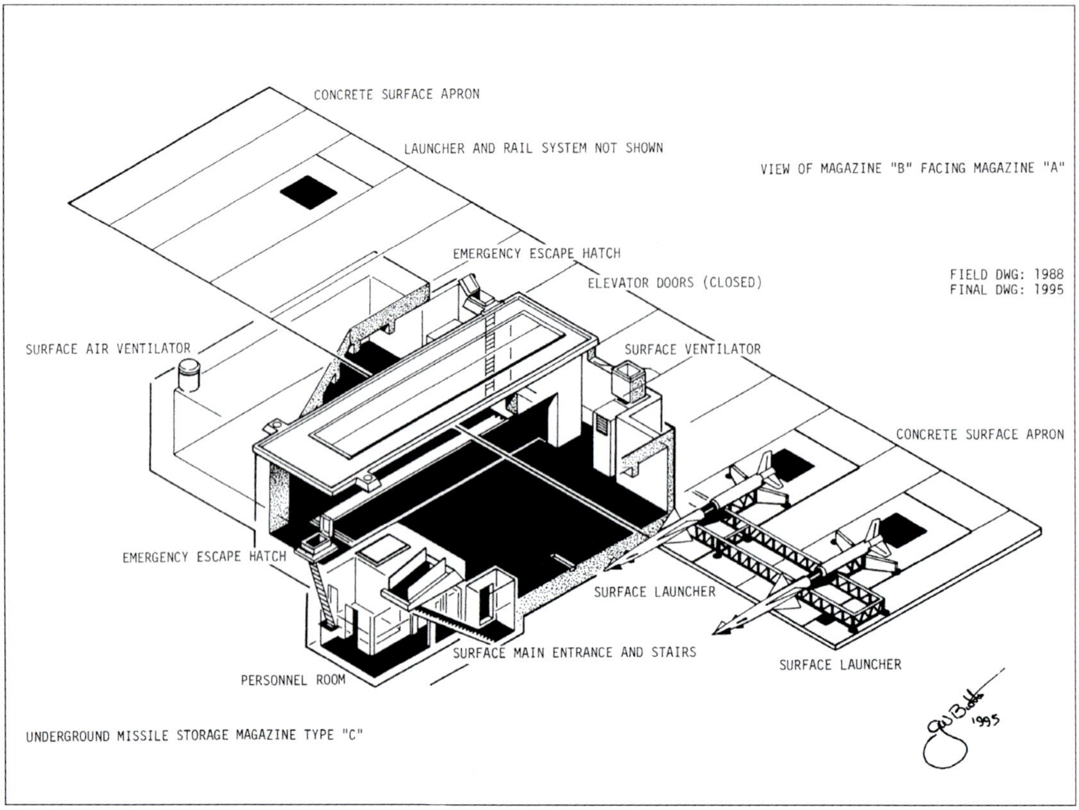

USMM: A phantom view of the Nahant Nike-Ajax Underground Storage Missile Magazine, of which three were constructed. Shown above is USMM design "C." The Nahant Nike site magazines were constructed of reinforced concrete with four feet thick walls and designated "A," "B," and "C" from west to east. Magazine 'A' was of the Type "B" design, while "B" and "C" magazines were type "C."

THE LAST MODIFICATIONS: In Fall 1957, extensive changes were made to the East Point Launcher Area, most of them being the physical launcher platforms and to upgrade electronic systems. The original layout of the launchers were affixed to a semi rectangular platform, surrounded by earth, as shown below. The new design incorporated rectangular pads, surrounded by paved asphalt. Remnants of the original rectangular launcher pad design may be viewed in the rocks below.

DRILL DRILL DRILL DRILL: Nahant Site B-17 was on alert status quite frequently, with an occasional "standown," for maintenance or relaxation. On pass, members of the battery were required "to return to their station within fifteen minutes." The top photograph depicts the magazine with a Nike-Ajax missile being readied to bring topside. Below is a typical magazine void of all missile apparatus.

MISSILE TEST AND ASSEMBLY BUILDING: This structure served as a facility to receive a missile from an Army depot, inspect, assemble and prepare the unit for installation of ammunition and refueling. Directly to the front of the building, a winding, concrete apron led to the refueling station. The upper image highlights a typical Missile Test and Assembly Building interior, while the lower photograph shows the Nahant exterior.

FUELLING: The Nike-Ajax missile was propelled by a three-finned booster that used a solid propellant. The missile, painted white in the Continental United States, consisted of three separate warheads of Composition "B." and fueled by a volatile chemical known as red fuming nitric acid and JP-4. Above is the station with personnel wearing protective suits and below as it appears today.

CARETAKER'S QUARTERS: The Caretaker's Quarters was situated nearly in line with Vernon Street and Swallow Cave Road. It was the secondary road into East Point and continued in a loop through to the main entrance at the end of Nahant Road. Following World War II through 1961, it was used as a Bachelor Officer's Quarters. Above: the quarters observed from Swallow Cave Road, and below, detail of the building and the front porch.

GENERATIONS!: A most unique capture. In the foreground of the upper image is the World War II Mess Hall; in the back is the Cold War dormitory for the Nike-Ajax missile system; and in the far left distance are the auxiliary structures from the original estate used as a Post Exchange, (P.X.) recreation and storage facility. Today, an aerial places the Mess Hall slab, center right, and the dormitory center left.

14

Marine Science Center

ACQUISITION: In the mid-1960s the Elliott cottage at East Point was set afire by vandals, represented by the lower images. Shortly thereafter, Northeastern University acquired East Point for research and to instruct students and professionals in the field of marine science. Proposals were then developed for the new school, but the initial action was to protect the site from vandals. Existing building adaptation soon followed.

THE BEGINNING: Upper image: Laboratory area from Battery 206 following demolition and debris removal. Mid-left is the former Elliott estate area. Bottom: Interior of enlisted men's dormitory following vandalism. Initial establishment at the Marine Science Institute in 1967 was overseen by Dr. Nathan Riser. Plans then began to create a world-worthy marine science learning and research center.

NEW SYSTEMS: The first Director at the Marine Science Center was Professor Nathan Riser, who in 1985, stood aside for Professor Ken Sebens. Major updates to the site took place, including the acquisition of the R/V *Mysis*. In 1991, the center was directed by Professor Joe Ayers. During this time, the military dormitory was greatly modified. Above is the Outdoor Mesocosm Facility, while below is a present overall capture.

NEW SYSTEMS II: In 2001, the next Director at the center was Professor Edward Jarroll through 2007, at which time Professor Gwilym Jones assumed directorship. In 2009, Professor Geoffrey C. Trussell became the next Director and remains so presently. Below, the area in 1953 from atop Battery Murphy looking at the former plotting room while the lower image was photographed in 1967.

TWO AERIAL CAPTURES IN TIME: The upper image clearly illustrates the conditions at the Marine Science Center in the late 1960s, following removal of buildings and scarifying of the grounds. The lower capture depicts the Center and grounds at present, including the addition of Lodge Park.

ACKNOWLEDGMENTS

This historical document of East Point, and the East Point Military Reservation, Nahant, Massachusetts, could not have been accomplished without the aid of Mrs. Alanna M. Butler-Guptil, and is also responsible for aerial scanning and finalizing imagery. Additional photographic assist was from Heather Ann Butler-Cook, Tara Maureen Butler, Emily A. Cook-Pauli, additional high aerial photography by David Morin. Doctor Geoff Trussell, Director at Northeastern University's Marine Science Center, was extremely helpful in this presentation allowing the photographers to access areas of East Point and the laboratories and Ryan Hill, who was tasked to open and photograph underground chambers for this work.

Early photographs were provided by the United States Army, Nahant Historical Society, Northeastern University archives and the author's personal collection. All illustrations were completed by the author.

It was a pleasure to work with my daughters, the Nahant Historical Society and Northeastern University on this historical project and, of course, Mr. Alan Sutton of Fonthill, and Arcadia Publishing.

Below is a remarkable late-February sunset image taken at the tip of East Point looking toward Boston.